Nature's Window

BUTTERFLIES

Sheila Buff

**Andrews McMeel
Publishing**

Kansas City

INTRODUCTION

One of summer's most charming sights is a sunny meadow filled with butterflies basking in the sun or gracefully fluttering from one flower to the next. Butterflies have been sipping nectar from flowering plants for the past forty million years—in fact, for as long as there have been flowering plants. They pay for their free meals by pollinating the flowers. Without butterflies and

Like all members of the Morphoidae family, the Ecuadorian morpho butterfly is a spectacular metallic blue; in this case, trimmed in pink. They are abundant in Central and South America.

other pollinating insects, there would be no flowers.

We have always been fascinated by the butterfly, especially its metamorphosis—the near-miraculous transformation from earthbound caterpillar to flying creature. The very first butterfly to appear in the spring is the orange or yellow butterfly of the sulphur family. Its vivid color—the same as fresh butter—may well be the origin of the English word butterfly.

Many of the world's most beautiful butterflies come from tropical regions. This tiger butterfly is found from Mexico to Brazil. Its antennae are unusually long and slender.

THE BUTTERFLY FAMILY

All butterflies are insects—that is, they have three distinct body regions (head, thorax, and abdomen), three pairs of jointed legs, one pair of antennae, and two sets of wings. Within the vast class of insects (about a million species), butterflies fall into the very large order called Lepidoptera. This word, which comes from the Greek words *lepidos*, meaning scales, and *pteros*, meaning wings, refers to the tiny scales that cover the wings of butterflies and give them

A typical butterfly, such as this poplar admiral, has two pairs of large wings—the forewings in front, the hindwings in back. Unlike most insects, butterflies can't fold their wings flat.

their incredibly varied and beautiful colors and patterns.

There are roughly 170,000 known Lepidoptera species—and more are discovered all the time, especially in the world's tropical regions. Almost all the Lepidoptera are moths. Only about 10 percent of the Lepidoptera, or about 17,000 species, are butterflies.

The difference between moths and butterflies is somewhat arbitrary, but generally speaking, moths fly at night and have drab colors, thicker bodies, and feathery antennae.

A pair of least skippers rests on a flower. Skippers are halfway between butterflies and moths. Their bodies are heavy, their colors dull, and their antennae end in curved clubs.

Butterflies fly during the day and are usually quite vividly colored, with slim bodies and thin antennae that end in a thickened area called a club.

Butterflies are found throughout the world, even in deserts and the icy Arctic; in fact, only Antarctica has no butterflies. One species, the Parnassian swallowtail, has been spotted at 13,500 feet on Mount Everest. Even so, the majority are found in tropical regions. About seven hundred species are regularly seen in the United States.

The swallowtails, with six thousand species, are the

biggest butterfly family and include the largest species. The world's largest butterfly is the female Queen Alexandra's birdwing, found only in Papua New Guinea. Its wingspan is an astonishing eleven inches, but despite its size this butterfly weighs less than an ounce. In North America, the largest butterfly is the two-tailed swallowtail, with a wingspan of four to six inches.

The world's smallest butterflies are found in North America. The pygmy blue and the dwarf blue both have wingspans of only about half an inch.

BUTTERFLY LIFE CYCLE

The life cycle of a butterfly is astonishingly complex and surprisingly short—as little as a few weeks. The process begins when a female butterfly mates with a male and then lays several hundred tiny eggs—one at a time—on plant leaves or stems. Exactly which plant is very important—most butterflies select one particular plant family, or even species, and no other. The monarch butterfly, for instance, selects only milkweed.

The eggs hatch in five to ten days. A tiny

After a female such as this European map butterfly (ARASCHNIA LEVANA) has mated, she seeks out a favored food plant and lays her eggs one at a time, usually on leaves.

The metamorphosis from caterpillar to butterfly is one of nature's most amazing miracles. Here a tiger butterfly caterpillar (right) prepares to pupate by attaching itself to the branch. A pupa nearly ready to emerge is at left.

caterpillar emerges and begins eating the leaves of its food plant. A caterpillar has six eyes on each side of its head, tiny antennae, and a small but strong mouth. Special glands on the bottom jaw, called spinnerets, produce silk. On the body right behind the head are three pairs of legs used for grasping; behind these are five pairs of soft, fleshy legs for moving.

Caterpillars eat voraciously and grow with amazing speed. Because a caterpillar's skin doesn't stretch as its body gets bigger, it must

A recently emerged poplar admiral butterfly clings to its pupal case. In the next hour or so, it will pump fluid into the veins of its damp, crumpled wings to make them expand.

molt, or shed its old skin, as it grows. Most caterpillars molt five times over a period of three to six weeks.

The final molt for a caterpillar occurs when it is a few weeks or even months old. For this molt, the caterpillar seeks out a protected place, often on or near its food plant. It uses silk from its spinnerets to attach itself firmly. Over the next day or so, a pupal skin forms beneath the caterpillar's skin. The outer skin then splits and the pupa, or chrysalis, is revealed. The chrysalis quickly hardens into a green or brown "case" in which the larva transforms, or metamorphoses, into an adult butterfly. The process generally takes about ten days to two weeks, although some species even spend the winter in chrysalis form and emerge early in the spring.

When the metamorphosis is complete, the pupal case splits open and the adult butterfly struggles out. It hangs upside down from the pupal case for an hour or so as its damp wings expand and harden. Then, its metamorphosis complete, the butterfly flies off to seek a mate and begin the process all over again.

*The viceroy butterfly,
widely found in North
America east of the Rockies,
is one of the first butterflies
seen when warm weather
arrives. This is because the
larvae hibernate over the
winter and emerge in the
early spring.*

BUTTERFLY BEHAVIOR

A newly emerged adult butterfly lives for only a few days or weeks. In that short time, it must find a mate and reproduce, all the while avoiding its many predators, especially birds.

Unlike most insects, butterflies don't have jaws. Instead, they have a strawlike proboscis, or feeding tube, for sucking nectar from flowers—the only food a butterfly consumes. When the proboscis isn't in use, it remains curled up under the mouth.

The white admiral is a member of the very large Nymphalidae, or brush-footed, family. The front pair of legs in these butterflies is undeveloped and can't be used for walking.

Male butterflies can sometimes be found gathered in large numbers near shallow puddles, damp ground, or mineral deposits. The males are puddling, or gathering minerals (especially salt) from the soil that have dissolved in the water. The males probably use the minerals to produce pheromones, scents that help attract females.

Butterflies employ a variety of strategies to find mates. Sometimes the males simply perch where they are likely to find a female—near a stream, for example—and fly out aggressively whenever

The stunning colors and intricate patterns of a butterfly's wings are made by millions of tiny, powdery scales that overlap in rows. Beneath the scales, the wings are clear.

anything resembling a female comes along. Another approach is to patrol an area likely to have females—a field containing the appropriate host plants for the caterpillars, for example. Hill-topping is another effective strategy. Both the males and females of a species fly upward toward the top of a hill, coming together at the crest. In wooded areas, butterflies of the same species tend to gather together in sunny clearings, a strategy known as lekking.

Butterflies fly best when their temperature

The scalloped wing edges and checkered or spotted pattern of this great spangled frittilary are typical of the family (the word frittilary means spotted). They are found in damp and marshy areas.

is at least 85 degrees Fahrenheit. Like all insects, however, they are cold-blooded and can't regulate their body temperature on their own. Instead, they bask in the sun to warm their bodies enough to fly. Most commonly, the butterfly basks by spreading its wings out and turning its back to the sun. Heat is absorbed by the butterfly's dark body and the part of the wings closest to the body.

Dried puddles leave dissolved minerals behind. These male tiger swallowtails are puddling, or absorbing the salty minerals. They need the salts to produce pheromones.

Butterflies also often bask with their wings closed and upright; the heat is absorbed by the dark area at the base of the hindwing.

*The black swallowtail
is a large butterfly
(its wingspan often
exceeds three inches)
found in gardens,
open fields, and
meadows east of the
Rockies.*

Butterflies avoid predators in a variety of ways. Many have large "eye spots" that fool enemies into thinking the defenseless butterfly is really a more formidable foe best left alone.

Some poisonous or bad-tasting butterflies have very vivid markings that serve as warnings to predators. Some butterfly species that don't taste bad have the same warning colors as those that do. This is a form of mimicry—predators avoid all butterflies with those colors.

Almost all members of the large swallowtail family have "tails" on their hindwings, as this black swallowtail does. Predators mistake the tail for the head and attack the wings, not the vulnerable body.

MONARCH MIGRATION

The monarch butterfly is the only insect in North America that migrates south and then north again every year. The fragile butterflies, with wingspans of only four inches, travel as much as twenty-five hundred miles to their wintering roosts in southern California and Mexico.

The amazing migration starts in the fall with the

The female monarch butterfly lays her eggs only on the milkweed plant. The caterpillars eat the milkweed leaves, absorbing toxins that make the species very distasteful to predators.

butterflies that emerged in late summer all over North America. Instead of mating, laying eggs, and dying, these butterflies head south, some-

Millions of monarchs crowd into a very small space in Mexico at the end of their long journey south. The monarchs are very selective and roost only at thirty densely wooded sites—sites that today are threatened by logging operations.

times gathering in large swarms as they do. Migrating monarchs can reach speeds of thirty miles per hour and have been spotted flying as much as a mile high.

Monarchs from east of the Rockies end up at a forty-mile section of the rugged, heavily forested mountains of Mexico just west of Mexico City. They roost in one of only thirty sites; so many butterflies arrive in the area that densities reach four million monarchs per acre. West of the Rockies, the monarchs migrate to southern California and roost in forested areas there.

In the early spring, the monarchs head north again. When they reach Texas and Louisiana, they mate, lay their eggs on milkweed plants, and die. The next generation heads north to the Great Lakes region, lays eggs, and dies. The generation or two after that spreads farther north and east. In the fall, the latest generation migrates south and begins the process all over again. How do the monarchs know precisely where to go and how to get there? The answer is still one of nature's great mysteries.

CONSERVATION AND PRESERVATION

Throughout the world today, butterflies are severely threatened by habitat loss and other hazards, such as pesticides and over-collection. Some are already extinct; others, especially those of the tropical rain forests, are in danger of becoming extinct before they even have been discovered. Currently, more than a hundred species are listed as vulnerable, endangered, or threatened. The dangers facing all thirteen members of the spectacular birdwing family are a good example.

This Cairn's birdwing and twelve other members of the birdwing family are the largest butterflies in the world. Native to the Indo-Australian region, they are threatened by habitat loss and over-collection.

Habitat destruction in the rain forests of Malaysia, Papua New Guinea, Indonesia, and elsewhere is the biggest concern, but over-collecting of the world's larger butterflies to meet the demand for specimens is also having a serious impact. Trade in these butterflies is restricted, but the laws are often ignored or circumvented.

The problem of habitat loss is not restricted to the rain forests of the tropics—creeping suburbanization is degrading and destroying habitats around the globe. Most butterflies live out their

Natural camouflage lets this butterfly in Malaysia hide by blending in with tree bark. Deforestation threatens the habitats of all the world's tropical butterflies.

lives in a very small world, sometimes no larger than an overgrown pasture full of wildflowers. If that field is bulldozed for another shopping mall, the genetic diversity of that butterfly colony is gone forever.

When habitat is saved or restored, the butterflies are saved as well. By restoring prairie habitat in Illinois for example, volunteers also brought back previously rare butterflies—proving once again that vigorous action by concerned individuals and organizations can have a powerful effect.

A flashy, iridescent blue, the large Ulysses butterfly of Australia is prized by collectors, who are willing to pay high prices. This species has been over-collected and is now protected.

Photography credits

All images provided by ENP Images except pages 38–39.

© Steve Gettle: pages 2, 10, 25, 28, 31, 32–33, 34; © Pete Oxford: pages 4, 7, 16–17;

© H.C. Kappel/BBC-NHU: pages 9, 15, 18; © Gerry Ellis: pages 22–23, 27, 37, 45;

© Jessie Harris: pages 38–39; © Konrad Wothe: pages 42, 47;

Front jacket: © H.C. Kappel/BBC-NHU;

Back jacket: © Pete Oxford.

www.andrewsmcmeel.com

ISBN: 0-8362-5299-3

Printed in Singapore

First U.S. edition

1   3   5   7   9   10   8   6   4   2

Editor: Deri Reed
Art Director: Tomek Lamprecht
Designer: Paola Pelosi

Produced by Smallwood & Stewart, Inc., New York City

My Little Blessings & Prayers
Prayer Book

CONCORDIA PUBLISHING HOUSE · SAINT LOUIS

Dearest Jesus, lead the way
Through the coming hours of day.
Keep me safe in all I do,
Ever close, my Lord, to You. Amen.

Adapted from *God's Children Pray*

For this new morning with its light,
Father, we thank Thee;
For rest and shelter of the night,
Father, we thank Thee;
For health and food, for love and friends,
For everything Thy goodness sends,
Father in heaven, we thank Thee. Amen.

Ralph Waldo Emerson (1803–82)

Lord,
Your hands fashioned and made me.
You have granted me life and steadfast love,
and Your care has preserved my spirit. Amen.
Job 10:8,12

Most merciful Redeemer,
Friend and Brother,
May we know You more clearly,
Love You more dearly,
And follow You more nearly,
Day by day. Amen.

Adapted from Richard of Chichester (1197–1253)

Our Father, who art in heaven,
hallowed be Thy name,
Thy kingdom come,
Thy will be done
on earth as it is in heaven.
Give us this day our daily bread;
and forgive us our trespasses
as we forgive those
who trespass against us;
and lead us not into temptation,
but deliver us from evil.
For Thine is the kingdom
and the power and the glory
forever and ever. Amen.

The Lord's Prayer

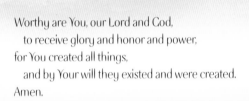

Worthy are You, our Lord and God,
   to receive glory and honor and power,
for You created all things,
   and by Your will they existed and were created.
Amen.

Revelation 4:11

10

I thank You, my heavenly Father, through Jesus Christ, Your dear Son, that You have kept me this night from all harm and danger; and I pray that You would keep me this day also from sin and every evil, that all my doings and life may please You. For into Your hands I commend myself, my body and soul, and all things. Let Your holy angel be with me, that the evil foe may have no power over me. Amen.

Martin Luther (1483–1546)

Let the words of my mouth
and the meditation of my heart
be acceptable in Your sight,
O LORD, my rock and my redeemer.

Psalm 19:14

12

For this new morning and its light,
For rest and shelter of the night,
For health and food,
For love and friends,
For everything Your goodness sends,
I thank You, heavenly Father. Amen.

From *Little Folded Hands*

13

Heavenly Father, hear my prayer:
Keep me in Your loving care.
Guard me through the coming day
In my work and in my play.
Keep me pure and strong and true.
Help me, Lord, Your will to do. Amen.

From *Little Folded Hands*

14

Oh come, let us sing to the LORD;
    let us make a joyful noise
        to the rock of our salvation!
Let us come into His presence
      with thanksgiving;
      let us make a joyful noise to Him
      with songs of praise!
For the LORD is a great God,
    and a great King above all gods.
In His hand are the depths
      of the earth;
    the heights of the mountains
      are His also.
The sea is His, for He made it,
    and His hands
      formed the dry land.

Oh come, let us worship and bow down;
    let us kneel before the LORD, our Maker!
For He is our God,
    and we are the people of His pasture,
    and the sheep of His hand.

Psalm 95:1–7

Praise God, from whom all blessings flow;
Praise Him, all creatures here below;
Praise Him above, ye heav'nly host:
Praise Father, Son, and Holy Ghost.

Thomas Ken (1637–1711)

17

Dear Savior, bless the children
Who've gathered here today;
Oh, send Your Holy Spirit,
And teach us how to pray.
Lord, bless all that we do here,
Oh, bless our gifts, though small.
And hear our prayer for Jesus' sake,
Who died to save us all. Amen.

From *Little Folded Hands*

18

Father God, I'm sorry
For the bad things that I do.
Forgive my sins and bless me.
In Jesus, make me new. Amen.

Lord, when we sin
(for there is no one who doesn't sin),
and we know it and are sorry,
and we ask You to forgive us,
please hear our prayer.
Listen from heaven,
and forgive us. In Jesus' name. Amen.

Solomon, 1 Kings 8:46–50

20

Loving Father,
You know everything about me.
You know when I'm good and when I'm not.
Please forgive me, God. Please help me
to make good choices and remember
to show Jesus' love to other people.
In His name I pray. Amen.

Watch o'er this little child tonight,
Blest Savior from above,
And keep me till the morning light
Within Thine arms of love. Amen.

From *Little Folded Hands*

22

The day is done;
O God the Son,
Look down upon
Thy little one!
O God of Light,
keep me this night,
And send to me
Thy angels bright.
I need not fear
if Thou art near;
Thou art my Savior,
kind and dear. Amen.

Adapted from Patty Caroline Dunsterville (1887)

23

Jesus, tender Shepherd, hear me;
Bless Thy little lamb tonight;
Through the darkness be Thou near me;
Watch my sleep till morning light. Amen.

Mary L. Duncan (1814–40)

24

Lord Jesus, keep me in Thy sight
Through the coming hours of night.
Then when morning sunlight beams
Wake me, Lord, from sleepy dreams. Amen.

From *God's Children Pray*

Incline Your ear, O LORD, and answer me,
    for I am poor and needy.
Preserve my life, for I am godly;
    save Your servant, who trusts in You—You are my God. Amen.

Psalm 86:1–2

Hear my prayer, O LORD,
  and give ear to my cry;
    hold not Your peace at my tears! Amen.

Psalm 39:12

God, take my hand and lead me
upon life's way;
Direct, protect, and feed me
from day to day;
Without Your grace and favor
I go astray
So take my hand, O Savior,
and lead the way. Amen.

Julie von Hausmann (1826–1901)

God, be in my head
and in my understanding.
God, be in my eyes
and in my looking.
God, be in my mouth
and in my speaking.
God, be in my mind
and in my thinking.
God, be at my end
and at my departing.

16th-Century Sarum Primer

28

I thank You, my heavenly Father, through Jesus Christ, Your dear Son, that You have graciously kept me this day; and I pray that You would forgive me all my sins where I have done wrong, and graciously keep me this night. For into Your hands I commend myself, my body and soul, and all things. Let Your holy angel be with me, that the evil foe may have no power over me. Amen.

Martin Luther (1483–1546)

Thank You, God,
  For making the world and all that is in it,
  For making my body and mind,
  For my home, my parents, and all the people
    who love and care for me,
  For food to eat and clothes to wear,
  For leading me to know Jesus, my Savior,
  For Baptism and the gifts of the Holy Spirit.
Thank You, God, for everything. Amen.

From *On-the-Go Prayers*

31

All good gifts around us
Are sent from heaven above.
Then thank the Lord,
O thank the Lord,
For all His love. Amen.
Matthias Claudius (1740–1815)

Be present at our table, Lord;
Be here and everywhere adored.
Thy children bless, and grant that we
May feast in paradise with Thee. Amen.
John Cennick (1718–55)

Come, Lord Jesus,
be our guest,
and let Thy gifts
to us be blessed. Amen.

To God who gives our daily bread
A thankful song we raise,
And pray that He who sends us food
May fill our hearts with praise. Amen.

Thomas Tallis (1505–85)

Ah, dearest Jesus, holy Child,
Prepare a bed, soft, undefiled,
A quiet chamber set apart
For You to dwell within my heart. Amen.

Martin Luther (1483–1546)

O holy Child of Bethlehem,
Descend to us, we pray;
Cast out our sin, and enter in,
Be born in us today.
We hear the Christmas angels
The great glad tidings tell;
O come to us, abide with us,
Our Lord Immanuel! Amen.

Phillips Brooks (1835–93)

35

I thank You, Jesus, for the night
And for the pleasant morning light,
For rest and food and loving care
And all that makes the world so fair.
Help me to do the things I should,
To be to others kind and good,
In all I do at work or play,
To grow more like You every day. Amen.

Adapted from *God's Children Pray*

36

God made the sun, and God made the tree;
God made the mountains, and God made me.
I thank You, O God, for the sun and the tree,
For making the mountains and for making me. Amen.

From *Little Folded Hands*

Your steadfast love, O LORD, extends to the heavens,
    Your faithfulness to the clouds.
Your righteousness is like the mountains of God;
    Your judgments are like the great deep;
man and beast You save, O LORD.
How precious is Your steadfast love, O God!
    The children of mankind take refuge in the shadow of Your wings. Amen.

Psalm 36:5–7

Dear Father, whom I cannot see,
Smile down from heaven on little me.
Let angels through the darkness spread
Their holy wings about my bed.
And keep me safe, because I am
The dear Good Shepherd's little lamb. Amen.

Adapted from *God's Children Pray*

Lord, keep us safe this night,
Secure from all our fears;
May angels guard us while we sleep,
Till morning light appears. Amen.

John Leland (1754–1841)

Teach me to love; teach me to pray.
Jesus above, teach me Your way.
Teach me how I, in my small way,
Can, with Your help, please You each day. Amen.

Adapted from *God's Children Pray*

At the close of every day,
Lord, to You, I kneel and pray.
Look upon Your little child.
Look in love and mercy mild.

Traditional

Now I lay me down to sleep,
I pray the Lord my soul to keep:
If I should die before I wake,
I pray the Lord my soul to take.
If I should live another day,
I pray the Lord to guide my way. Amen.

Traditional

Lord, I know that You are near,
in darkness and in light.
Thank You for being there
to care for me tonight.
Bethan James

41

Be near me, Lord Jesus;
I ask Thee to stay
Close by me forever
And love me, I pray.
Bless all the dear children
In Thy tender care,
And take us to heaven
To live with Thee there.

Anonymous

Lighten our darkness,
Lord, we pray,
and in Your great mercy
defend us from all the dangers of this night,
for the love of Jesus, Your only Son.

Traditional

43

We thank You, Lord God, heavenly Father, for all Your benefits, through Jesus Christ, our Lord, who lives and reigns with You and the Holy Spirit, now and forever. Amen.

Traditional

The LORD bless you
   and keep you;
the LORD make His face
   to shine upon you
   and be gracious to you;
the LORD lift up His countenance upon you
   and give you peace.

Numbers 6:24–26

May the peace of God,
which passes all understanding,
keep our hearts and minds
in the knowledge and love of God,
and of His Son, Jesus Christ, our Lord;
and the blessing of God Almighty,
the Father, the Son, and the Holy Spirit,
be with us and remain with us always. Amen.

The Blessing